513
Sch

Schwartz, David M.

If you hopped like
a frog

DATE DUE			

IF YOU HOPPED LIKE A FROG

BY David M. Schwartz

ILLUSTRATED BY James Warhola

SCHOLASTIC PRESS · NEW YORK

To all the creative, math-loving teachers who give me inspiration —
and especially to Kim Shepherd of Dallas, who gave me this idea! — D.S.

For Oonagh — J.W.

Library of Congress Cataloging-in-Publication Data
Schwartz, David M.
If you hopped like a frog / by David M. Schwartz; illustrated by James Warhola.
Summary: Introduces the concept of ratio by comparing what humans
would be able to do if they had bodies like different animals.
ISBN 0-590-09857-8
1. Ratio and proportion—Juvenile literature. [1. Ratio and proportion.
2. Anatomy, Comparative.] I. Warhola, James, ill. II. Title.   p.   cm.
QA117.S35 1999   513.2'4—dc21   98-46546   CIP   AC

10 9 8 7 6 5 4   0/0 01 02 03 04

Printed in Mexico   49
First edition, September 1999

The display type was set in Countryhouse.
The text type was set in 19-point Elroy.
Book design by David Caplan

Dear Reader,

When I was your age, most of my friends wanted to be astronauts, athletes, or actors. I, too, dreamed of traveling in space, hitting home runs, and starring in movies. But there was something else I wanted to do. I never told anyone.

I wanted to hop like a frog.

I imagined soaring through the air with grace and ease, landing gently on my big, springy legs. How far could I hop?

I also wanted to eat like a snake. A snake can open its jaws so wide that it can swallow prey wider than its head! I knew it would be very bad table manners to eat things bigger than my head. Still, I wondered what I could swallow if I swallowed like a snake.

When I realized that answering these questions took just a little bit of math, I had great fun astonishing my family and friends. Once you know that a frog can jump twenty times its body length, you can figure out how far you could hop if you hopped like a frog. When you realize a snake swallows food twice as wide as its head, you can find out what you could eat if you snacked like a snake. In fact, there is no limit to what you can figure out. . . . It's simply a matter of math!

Hop to it!

Your friend,

David

If you hopped like a FROG . . .

. . . you could jump
from home plate
to first base in
one mighty leap!

If you were as strong as an ANT...

. . . you could lift a car!

If you had the brain of a BRACHIOSAURUS...

. . . your brain
would be
smaller
than a
pea!

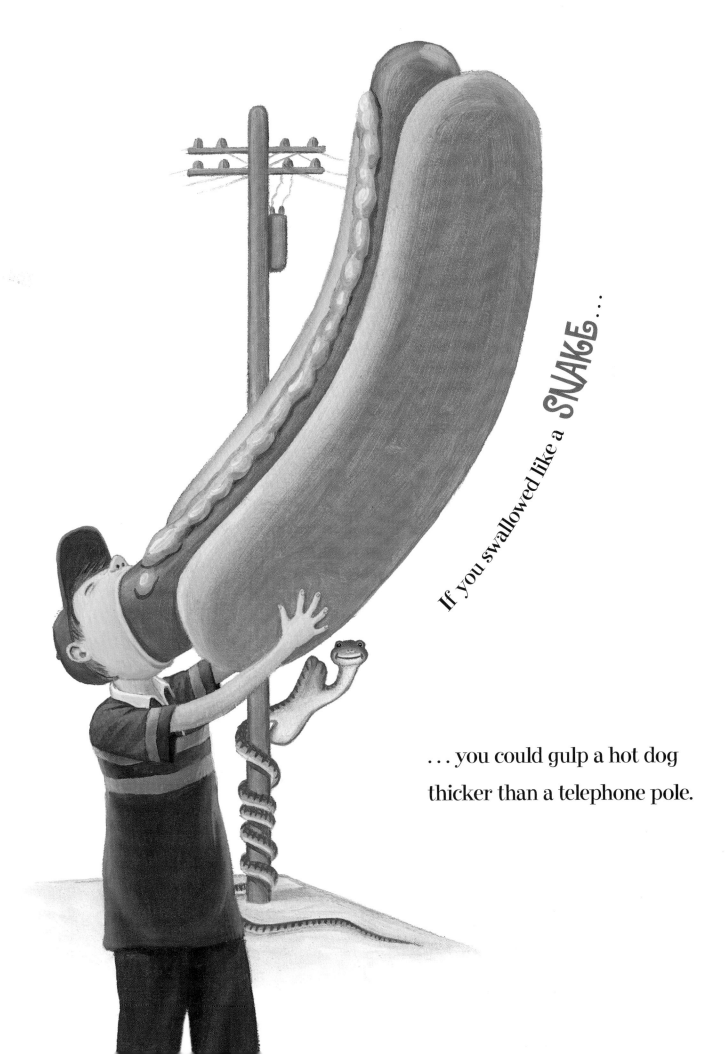

If you swallowed like a SNAKE...

... you could gulp a hot dog thicker than a telephone pole.

If you ate like a SHREW . . .

. . . you could
devour over 700
hamburgers in a day!

If you high-jumped like a FLEA...

. . . you could

land on Lady

Liberty's torch!

If you flicked your tongue like a CHAMELEON...

... you could whip the food off your plate without
using your hands! But what would your mother say?

If you craned your neck like a CRANE...

... you'd have
to stretch
your arm
w-a-a-ay up
to scratch
your head!

If you had EAGLE EYES...

. . . you could spot a
running rabbit
from high in the clouds!

If you dined like a PELICAN...

. . . you could slurp a
triple root beer float
in one mouthful!

If you grew as fast in your

FIRST NINE MONTHS

as you did in the nine months

BEFORE YOU WERE BORN...

. . . you would have been a

tot,

taller

than mountain tops . . .

and

heavier

than 2 ½ million elephants!

If you scurried like a SPIDER . . .

. . . you could charge down
an entire football field
in just two seconds!

If you hugged like a

BEAR...

... wait a minute — you already do!

If You Hopped Like a Frog . . .

Frogs are champion jumpers. A 3-inch frog can hop 60 inches. That means the frog is jumping 20 times its body's length. Let's suppose you are 4 $\frac{1}{2}$ feet tall. If you, like a frog, could hop 20 times your body length (your height), you would be able to sail from home plate to first base, 90 feet in all! *How tall are you? If you could jump 20 times your body length, how far could you go? Measure your height and multiply by 20 to find out!*

If You Were as Strong as an Ant . . .

Ants may be tiny, but they are great weight lifters. An ant weighing $\frac{1}{250}$ of an ounce can easily lift a bread crumb weighing $\frac{1}{5}$ of an ounce. That means the ant is lifting 50 times its own weight. If you weighed 60 pounds and you could lift 50 times your own weight, you would be able to lift a car weighing 3,000 pounds, or 1 $\frac{1}{2}$ tons! *How much do you weigh? If you could lift 50 times your weight, could you lift a 3,000-pound car? What else could you lift?*

If You Had the Brain of a *Brachiosaurus* . . .

Large dinosaurs had tiny brains. *Brachiosaurus* weighed about 80,000 kilograms, but its brain weighed only about 200 grams (0.2 kilograms). So its body was about 400,000 times as heavy as its brain. That means its brain weighed only $\frac{1}{400,000}$ as much as its body. If you had the brain of a *Brachiosaurus* and you weighed 30 kilograms, your brain would weigh $\frac{1}{400,000}$ of that, or 0.075 grams — far less than the weight of a pea! *What is your weight in kilograms? What would your brain weigh if it weighed $\frac{1}{400,000}$ as much as your body?*

If You Swallowed Like a Snake . . .

Your lower jaw is hinged to your upper jaw, but a snake's jaw is not. If a snake wants to eat something big, it can simply drop its entire lower jaw to get its mouth w–i–d–e open. That's how it swallows prey that seems gigantic. A Western diamondback rattlesnake with a head just 1 inch wide can swallow a whole gopher measuring 2 inches across. That means the snake is eating something twice as wide as its head! If your head were 5 inches across from ear to ear and you swallowed like a snake, you could gulp down something 10 inches thick — like a telephone pole! *How big is your head? What could you swallow if you swallowed something twice as big as your head?*

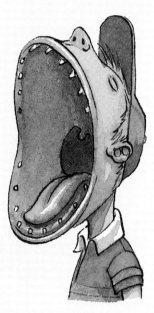

If You Ate Like a Shrew . . .

Shrews are among the smallest of mammals, but their appetites sure are huge! A shrew that weighs just $\frac{1}{5}$ of an ounce eats about $\frac{3}{5}$ of an ounce of yummy insects and worms each day. That means it eats 3 times its own weight daily! If you weighed 60 pounds and you gobbled up 3 times your weight in a day, you would eat 180 pounds of food. That's 720 quarter-pound hamburgers! *What would you eat if you ate 3 times your weight?*

If You High-jumped Like a Flea . . .

A flea just 3 millimeters high can spring more than 200 millimeters into the air — almost 70 times its own height. That's how it latches on to dogs, cats, and other warm-blooded animals. The flea can jump this way because its muscles contain the world's springiest substance, resilin. If you could jump 70 times your height and you were 135 centimeters tall, you would be able to leap almost 95 meters into the air, which would easily get you onto the torch of the Statue of Liberty, 93 meters above the ground. *Measure your height in centimeters and figure out how high you'd go if you could jump 70 times your height. Could you land on the Statue of Liberty? What are some of the things you could jump over or onto?*

If You Flicked Your Tongue Like a Chameleon . . .

Old World chameleons are experts at standing still, unnoticed by unlucky insects. When one flies by, . . . *Zzzzzap!* Out goes a very long tongue. *Gotcha!* The fly is now food.

A 1-foot chameleon may have a 6-inch tongue. Its tongue is half as long as its body. If you had the tongue of a chameleon and you were 4 feet 6 inches (54 inches) tall, your tongue would be 2 feet 3 inches (27 inches) long. You could sit at the table and pick up your food with your tongue. *How long would your tongue be if you had a tongue like a chameleon's?*

If You Craned Your Neck Like a Crane . . .

One look at a crane and you'll understand the expression "crane your neck." A whooping crane that's 4 feet tall (48 inches) has a 16-inch neck. That means its neck is $\frac{1}{3}$ the height of its body. If your neck were $\frac{1}{3}$ of your height and you were 4 feet 6 inches (54 inches) tall, your neck would be 18 inches long — about as long as your arms. So your head would be an arm's length above your shoulders! *How tall are you? How long would your neck be if it were $\frac{1}{3}$ your height?*

If You Had Eagle Eyes . . .

Deep inside the eye, on a surface called the retina, are many tiny cells called cones. The more cones an eye has, the sharper its vision. You have about 200,000 cones on each square millimeter of your retina. Eagles have about 1,000,000 cones in the same area. So an eagle has about 5 times as many cones. It sees about 5 times as well as you do. From the air, you can spot a moving rabbit about 300 meters away. With eagle eyes, you could spot it 5 times as far as that — about 1,500 meters (or 1.5 kilometers) away. That would put you into the clouds. *Measure (or estimate) 1,500 meters. What can you see from that distance?*

If You Dined Like a Pelican . . .

The enormous sac that hangs from a pelican's bill can hold 3 gallons of water, but only 1 gallon can fit into its stomach, so the bird can't gulp down everything it takes into its pouch. It squirts out most of the water and swallows the fish left behind. Your own stomach can hold about 1 pint. So if you, like a pelican, had a pouch that could hold three times as much as its stomach, you could slurp three 16-ounce root beer floats. Like the pelican, you wouldn't be able to swallow it all. You'd have to spit out most of the root beer in order to swallow the ice cream. *What else could you slurp if you dined like a pelican?*

If You Grew as Fast in Your First Nine Months as You Did in the Nine Months Before You Were Born . . .

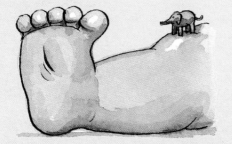

You may think you're growing fast now, but it's slow compared to how fast you grew before you were born! You started out as a fertilized egg weighing less than 35 billionths of an ounce. At birth you might have weighed about 7 ½ pounds, or 120 ounces. Your weight increased about 3 ½ billion times inside your mother's womb! If your weight increased another 3 ½ billion times in the nine months *after* you were born, you would have weighed about 26 billion pounds (or 13 million tons) by the time you were 9 months old! That's more than the weight of 100,000 blue whales or 2 ½ million elephants! How tall would you have been? When you were just a fertilized egg, you were about .004 inches in diameter. By the time you were born, you were probably about 20 inches in length. Your length increased 5,000 times. If it increased another 5,000 times in the nine months after you were born, you would have been 100,000 inches, or 8,333 feet, over 1 ½ miles tall. That's higher than many mountains. *Find out your weight and length at birth. If you continued to grow at your pre-birth rate, how heavy and tall would you be now?*

If You Scurried Like a Spider . . .

Considering its length, a female house spider is faster than any other animal, even a chee-tah. It can move 33 times the length of its own body in 1 second! If you could do that and you were 4 feet 6 inches tall, you could move about 150 feet per second. That means that in two seconds, you could run 300 feet, or 100 yards — the entire length of a football field! That's about 5 times faster than the speed of a champion Olympic runner! *If you could run 33 times your body length in a second, how many feet per second could you run? How long would it take you to run the length of a 100-yard football field? How far could you run in a minute if you could keep up that pace?*